NATIONAL
GEOGRAPHIC
KiDS

Weird but true!

3

350 OUTRAGEOUS FACTS

NATIONAL GEOGRAPHIC

WASHINGTON, D.C.

Octopuses
have
three
hearts.

THE UNIVERSE IS ABOUT 13.7 BILLION YEARS OLD.

KANGAROOS CAN JUMP MORE THAN 30 FEET (9 m) IN ONE HOP. THAT'S THE LENGTH OF 12 SKATEBOARDS!

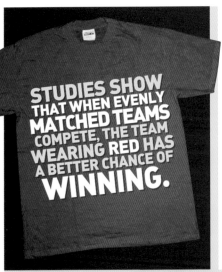

STUDIES SHOW THAT WHEN EVENLY MATCHED TEAMS COMPETE, THE TEAM WEARING RED HAS A BETTER CHANCE OF WINNING.

One of the shortest wars ever lasted 38 MINUTES.

There was a **hotel** made of **garbage** in Rome, Italy.

LEMONS CAN HAVE MORE SUGAR THAN STRAWBERRIES.

The Earth spins so fast that someone standing at the

Equator is traveling at about 1,000 miles an hour.

(1,600 km/h)

9

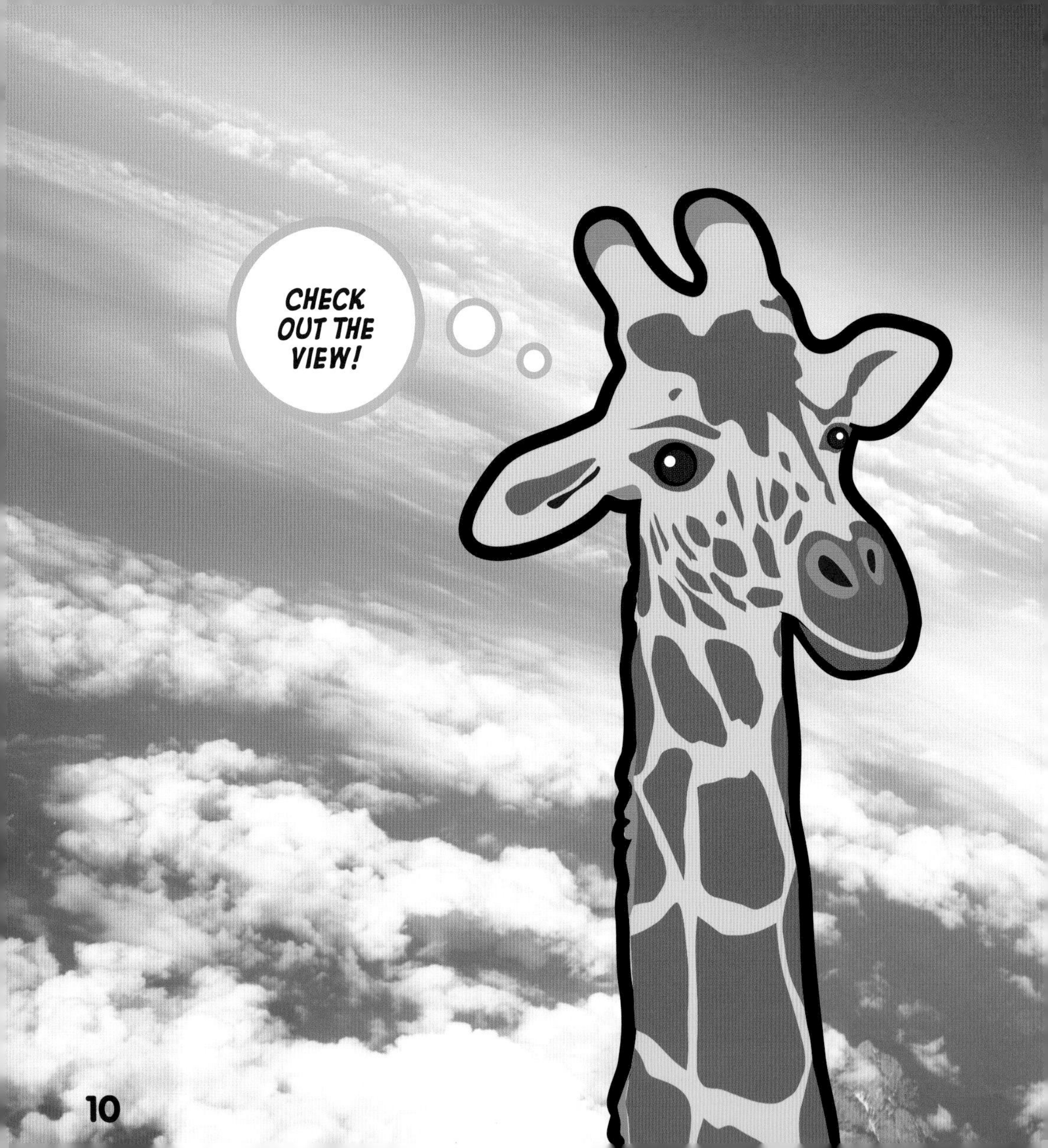
CHECK OUT THE VIEW!

It would take a stack of more than 100,000 giraffes to reach the outermost layer of the Earth's atmosphere.

The Earth weighs about 6,600,000,000,000,000,000,000,000 metric tons.

(1 metric ton=2,204.6 pounds)

Legend says that Aztec ruler **Moctezuma** drank 50 cups of hot chocolate a day.

ELEPHANTS CAN RUN FASTER THAN HUMANS.

YOU LOSE UP TO 100 HAIRS A DAY.

A warm frog makes faster croaking noises than a cold frog.

THE FIRST AIRPLANE JOURNEY ACROSS THE UNITED STATES TOOK 49 DAYS.

SEEING THE COLOR RED CAN MAKE YOUR HEART BEAT FASTER.

SOME **DIAMONDS** ARE MORE THAN A **BILLION YEARS OLD.**

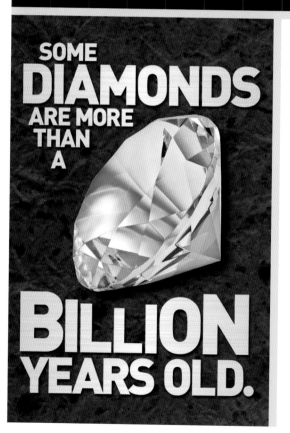

IT'S **POSSIBLE** TO PRODUCE ELECTRICITY FROM **ELEPHANT DUNG.**

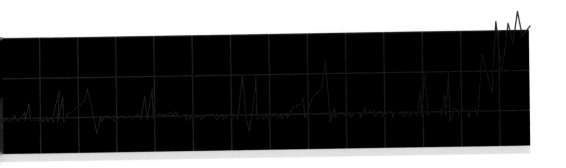

IF HUMANS CAME IN AS MANY SIZES AS DOGS, WE'D RANGE FROM **THREE** TO **EIGHTEEN** FEET TALL.

(91.4 cm to 5.5 m)

Some astronauts living on the Mir space station ate Jell-O every Sunday to help keep track of the days.

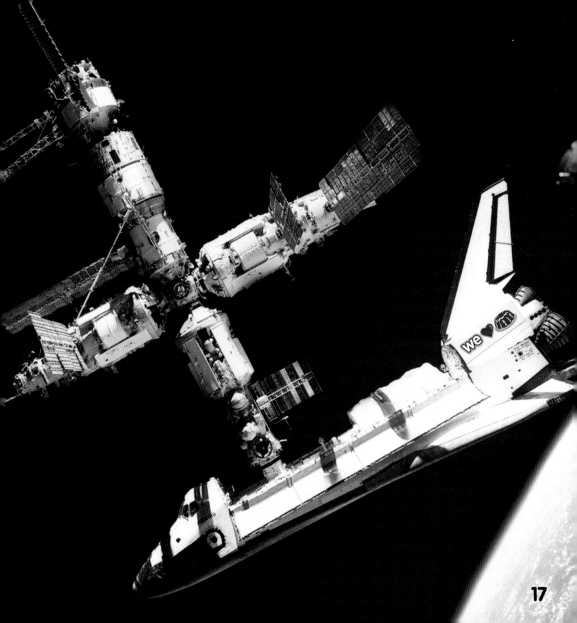

AN AVERAGE MAJOR LEAGUE **BASEBALL** IS USED FOR ONLY SIX PITCHES.

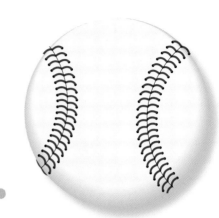

YOUR FEET HAVE 500,000 SWEAT GLANDS.

SAUCER-SHAPED LENTICULAR CLOUDS HAVE BEEN MISTAKEN FOR UFOS.

ALL THE
MINED GOLD
IN THE WORLD
CAN FILL TWO
OLYMPIC-SIZE
SWIMMING POOLS.

A
man once ate
49 glazed
doughnuts
in
8 minutes.

More than a thousand Earths could fit inside Jupiter.

IF YOU TRAVELED AS FAST AS A CAR ON THE HIGHWAY, IT WOULD TAKE NEARLY THREE DAYS AND NIGHTS TO REACH THE EARTH'S CORE.

DAYS WERE ONLY 18 HOURS LONG A BILLION YEARS AGO.

THERE ARE **HUNDRED-FOOT-TALL** (30 m) SAND DUNES IN ALASKA.

A queen bee can lay **2,000** eggs a day in the spring.

SCORPIONS GLOW UNDER BLACK LIGHT.

A woman's **heart** usually beats faster than a man's **heart**.

It's impossible to see a full rainbow in the sky at noon.

Some **FROGS** survive the winter by freezing almost solid.

Four-thousand-
year-old popcorn

was found
in a cave
in New Mexico, U.S.A.

A lizard
sticks its tongue out
to smell.

FAN FACT! SUBMITTED BY BEN D., 9

In Italy, you can buy

fresh pizza

from a
vending machine.

SATURN'S RINGS ARE MADE OF ICE AND ROCKS.

A gold-plated bicycle sold for £80,000 ($125,344) in the U.K.

Sperm whales have the heaviest BRAINS on the planet.

A cat has about **20** muscles in each ear.

Certain sharks walk on their fins **underwater.**

LOOKS LIKE A NICE DAY FOR A STROLL!

Some moths drink the tears of elephants.

33

In the summer, the amount of water pouring over Niagara Falls (on the U.S.-Canada border) each second could fill 13,000 bathtubs.

Your brain is about three-quarters water.

Frog bones grow new rings as they age, just like trees.

Dirty snow melts faster than clean snow.

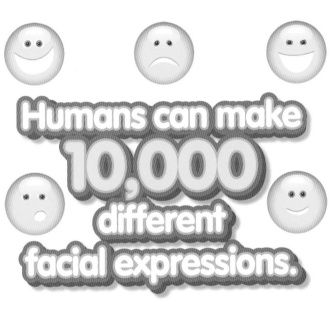

Humans can make 10,000 different facial expressions.

THE OLDEST ROCKS IN THE GRAND CANYON ARE ALMOST TWO BILLION YEARS OLD.

Cheetah ancestors roamed North America about four million years ago.

Every zebra's stripe pattern is different.

THE CORPSE FLOWER GROWS UP TO 12 FEET TALL (3.7 m) AND SMELLS LIKE ROTTING MEAT.

WHAT STINKS?

40

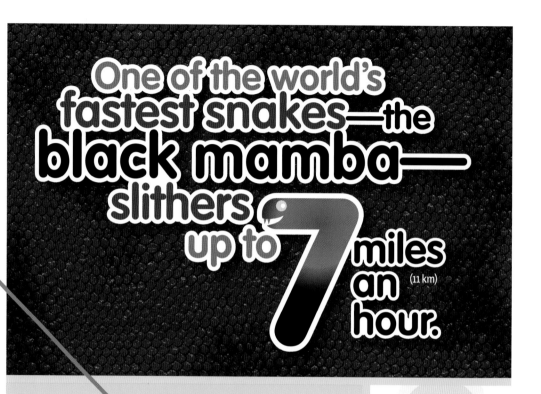

One of the world's fastest snakes—the **black mamba**—slithers up to **7** miles **an hour.** (11 km)

A MALE AFRICAN CICADA CAN MAKE **A SOUND AS LOUD** AS A POWER MOWER.

A RIPE CRANBERRY WILL **BOUNCE.**

A company once sold a **cupcake-shaped** designer handbag— with strawberry- and-chocolate- colored crystals— **for $4,295.**

There is a **40**-FOOT (12-m)-tall steel statue of a **PRAYING MANTIS** that SHOOTS FLAMES from its ANTENNAE in downtown Las Vegas, Nevada, U.S.A.

A man spent **93 DAYS PADDLEBOARDING 4,000 MILES** from Africa to the Caribbean. (6,500 km)

You can get your **SELFIE** turned into **LATTE ART.**

NASA is designing a new fabric for astronauts that looks like the **CHAIN MAIL MEDIEVAL KNIGHTS WORE.**

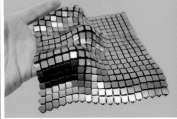

A museum in Alaska, U.S.A., features an **OUTHOUSE** made of **ICE.**

A Japanese cat owner **MAKES HATS** for her pets **USING THEIR OWN FUR.**

44

Reading the word **"SUN"** can cause your **PUPILS TO GET SMALLER.**

BAMBOO SHARKS shrug their shoulders to help them **SWALLOW FOOD.**

Some **CLOUDS** are filled with **LOLLIPOP-SHAPED ICE CRYSTALS.**

An asparagus spear can grow **10 inches** (25 cm) in **24 hours.**

You can buy a **TENNIS-BALL-SIZE STRAWBERRY** in Japan for **$4,000.**

That's Weird!

AN ELEVATOR IN GERMANY can travel up and down, side to side, and diagonally.

IT IS **ILLEGAL** to have a **PET RAT** in Alberta, Canada.

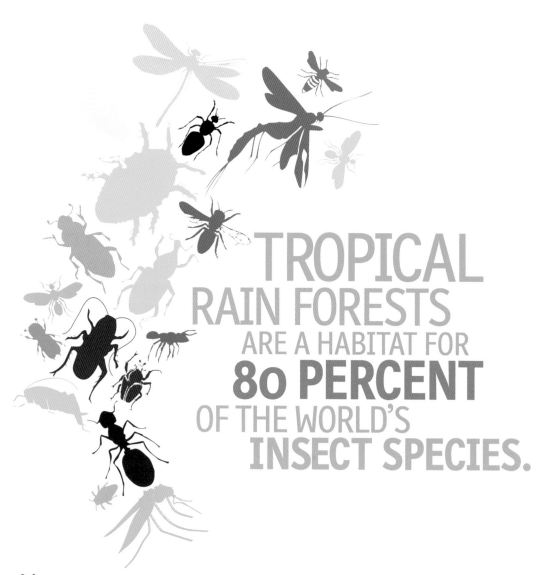

TROPICAL
RAIN FORESTS
ARE A HABITAT FOR
80 PERCENT
OF THE WORLD'S
INSECT SPECIES.

Mummies of ancient **Egyptian royalty** were wrapped in thousands of feet (meters) of bandages.

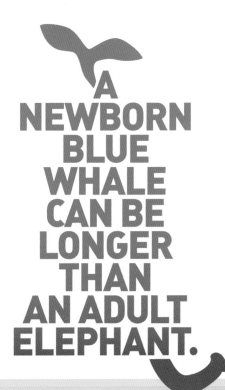

A NEWBORN BLUE WHALE CAN BE LONGER THAN AN ADULT ELEPHANT.

A camel's eye has eyelids.

EVERY CONTINENT HAS A CITY CALLED ROME (EXCEPT ANTARCTICA).

Newborn dolphins sleep for only a few seconds at a time.

49

Earth's
temperature
rises slightly
during a full
moon.

MOUNT
EVEREST
IS ABOUT
27
TIMES
TALLER
THAN THE
EIFFEL
TOWER.

Yawns are contagious for **chimpanzees,** just as they are for **humans.**

Every (6.5 sq cm) **square inch of your skin** hosts about 6 million bacteria.

BUTTERFLIES MUST WARM THEIR WINGS IN THE SUN BEFORE FLYING.

Guinea pigs can walk as soon as they are born.

FAN FACT! SUBMITTED BY ALEC S., 11

Your stomach would digest itself without mucus.

An eagle's nest can s t r e t c h wider than your sofa.

The world's longest known crystal is 37.4 feet long. (11.4 m) That's 8 times taller than an average 10-year-old.

HUMANS have lived on Earth for about **200,000** years; **DINOSAURS** walked the planet for roughly *160 million* years.

MORE THAN
99 PERCENT
OF THE SPECIES THAT
HAVE EVER EXISTED ARE NOW
EXTI

NCT.

**Olive oil** and **garlic** are **real ice-cream flavors.**

*Some pet spas serve catnip tea to feline guests.*

Spit can *freeze in midair* at the **North Pole.**

 **LAIKA THE DOG WAS THE FIRST**
 **"ASTRONAUT" TO TRAVEL INTO SPACE.**

THERE ARE
**ABOUT
3,000**
LIGHTNING
FLASHES
ON
EARTH
EVERY MINUTE.

SKUNKS HAVE STRIPED SKIN UNDER THEIR FUR.

Blondes have more hairs on their heads than brunettes.

THE BIGGEST KNOWN INTACT DINOSAUR SKULL

THE FIRST **SPACE TOURIST PAID** **$20 MILLION** FOR A TEN-DAY TRIP TO THE INTERNATIONAL SPACE STATION.

BOUQUETS IN AUSTRIA HAVE AN ODD NUMBER OF **FLOWERS;** EVEN NUMBERS ARE CONSIDERED **BAD LUCK.**

IS L O N G E R THAN A **RACEHORSE'S BODY.**

The **bombardier beetle** can shoot hot **poison** from its rear end **500** times a second.

More men are color-blind than women.

Some **sea stars** break off their own arms **when frightened.**

YIKES!

The largest known ant supercolony stretches **nearly 4,000 miles** (6,440 km) **through Portugal, Spain, France, and Italy.**

The Hawaiian alphabet has only **13** letters.

YOU CAN BUY FAKE EYEBROWS AND EYELASHES MADE OUT OF REAL **HAIR.**

THE HARDER YOU CONCENTRATE, **THE LESS YOU BLINK.**

Crocodiles
sometimes
walk on the backs of hippos.

A river in
Canada
once turned
red.

SHALOM HEI BAREV KUMUSTA SALAAM KIA ORA
APA KHABAR NI HAO HALLO ZDRAVO
BONJOUR GOEDENDAG HUJAMBO HEI SA'LAM
YIA SOU
MBOTE **Nearly** TIENA YISTILIGN MINGALA BA
AHOJ! BOM DIA SOUR SDEY
BOK XIN CHÀO
AHLAN WA SAHLAN **7,000** JÓ NAPOT
AKWAABA DIA DHUIT
MONI **languages** MALO
ANNYONG HASEYO SALEM
LABAS HOLA **are spoken** TERVIST
SABBAI DII SAIN BAINA UU
MERHABA **worldwide.** OI
VITAYU HALLÓ JAMA NGAA CZEŚĆ WHAH GWAAN
PRIVYET JAMBO KONNICHI WA HEJ
SAWATDEE BUNĂZIUA E KARO GRÜTSIE
NAMASTE
CIAO MHOROI MBA'ÉICHAPA ASSALAMO ALAIKUM

68

ONE OF THE **WORLD'S LARGEST BUILDINGS** SITS ON A FAULT LINE IN TAIWAN; ITS WEIGHT MAY HAVE TRIGGERED SEVERAL EARTH-QUAKES.

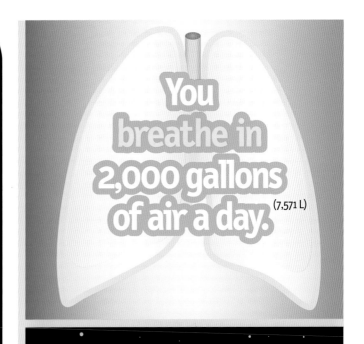

You breathe in 2,000 gallons of air a day. (7,571 L)

The world's largest menorah is taller than a three-story building.

MALE WOODCHUCKS ARE CALLED HE-CHUCKS;

FEMALES ARE CALLED SHE-CHUCKS.

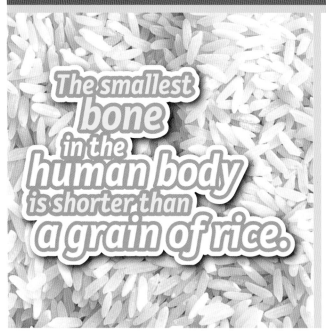

The smallest **bone** in the **human body** is shorter than **a grain of rice.**

CAMELS CHEW IN A FIGURE-EIGHT MOTION.

The **oldest chocolate** ever found was inside a **2,600-year-old pot** in Belize.

STUDIES SHOW THAT PAINTING YOUR ROOM **BLUE** COULD MAKE YOU MORE CREATIVE.

A SHARK CAN LIVE FOR SIX WEEKS WITHOUT EATING.

71

THE WORLD'S POPULATION GROWS BY ABOUT A BILLION PEOPLE EVERY 12 YEARS.

Small icebergs are called growlers and bergy bits.

There was once
a lake
the size of England
in the Sahara.

BLING!
BLING!

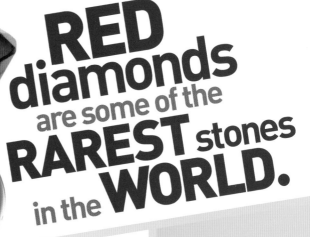

RED diamonds are some of the **RAREST** stones in the **WORLD.**

WARTHOGS DON'T **HAVE** **WARTS.**

SALT HAS BEEN USED AS MONEY.

THE SUN IS **400** TIMES LARGER THAN THE **MOON.**

Mantis shrimp can see colors better than humans can.

Australian Aboriginals, *the world's oldest living culture,* have existed for at least 50,000 years.

astro h2o

Astronauts drink recycled urine.

A METEORITE ONCE HIT A MAILBOX IN GEORGIA, U.S.A.

Parrots talk without vocal cords.

HAIR GROWS ALMOST **EVERYWHERE** ON YOUR **SKIN** EXCEPT YOUR LIPS, THE PALMS OF YOUR HANDS, AND THE SOLES OF YOUR FEET.

Months that begin on **SUNDAYS** always have a Friday the 13th.

Rats can't **b u r p.**

TEST FLIGHTS OF THE **FIRST SPACE SHUTTLE** TOOK OFF FROM THE **BACK OF A FLYING 747.**

Scientists think substances found in **SEAWEED** could be used to **EXTEND THE LIFE OF CELL PHONE BATTERIES.**

A 400-YEAR-OLD SILK DRESS was recently **RECOVERED FROM A SHIPWRECK** in the North Sea.

The force of a **COCONUT CRAB'S PINCH** is stronger than **CRUSHING YOUR TOE** under a **REFRIGERATOR.**

A coffee-pot-shaped water tower in California, U.S.A., could hold the equivalent of **1.28 MILLION CUPS OF COFFEE.**

WHEN SEAHORSES ARE ANGRY, THEY "GROWL."

A model of the **GREEK PARTHENON** on display in Germany is made of **STEEL, PLASTIC, AND 100,000 BANNED BOOKS.**

The **LIGHTS ON A BRIDGE** in Montreal, Canada, **CHANGE COLOR** at night **based on the day's weather, traffic, and news.**

There is a **WORLD** championship for best **LATTE ART.**

A GLASS-BOTTOM INFINITY POOL HANGS OFF A BUILDING **500 FEET** (152 m) ABOVE A STREET IN HOUSTON, TEXAS, U.S.A.

THE WORLD'S LONGEST MARBLE RUN was **6,293 FEET** (1,918 m) and **STRETCHED ACROSS A SMALL TOWN IN SWITZERLAND.**

A nearly **2,000-year-old loaf of bread** was found during excavations of **Italy's Mount Vesuvius.**

An **ELEPHANT SEAL** can recognize a rival by the **TEMPO** of its **CALL.**

That's Weird!

85

Dolphins may be smarter

than chimpanzees.

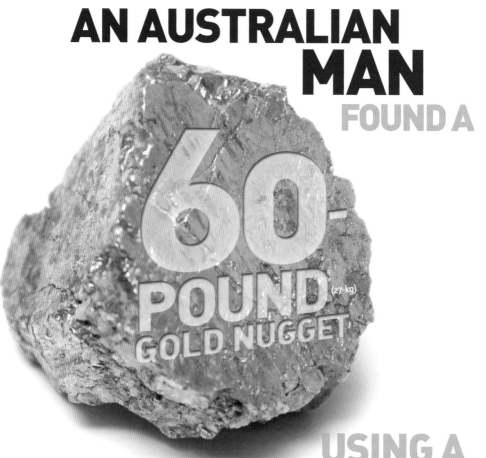

AN AUSTRALIAN MAN FOUND A

60-POUND (27-kg) GOLD NUGGET

USING A METAL DETECTOR.

Chromophobia is the extreme fear of colors.

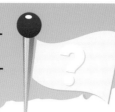

No country owns ANTARCTICA.

AT A RESTAURANT IN MICHIGAN, U.S.A., YOU CAN ORDER A SUPERSIZE HAMBURGER THAT WEIGHS AS MUCH AS A GROWN MAN.

Most spiders have

8

eyes.

Most swans in England belong to the Queen.

SOME PEOPLE CAN HEAR THEIR EYEBALLS MOVING.

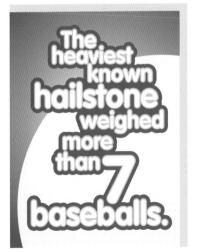

The heaviest known hailstone weighed more than 7 baseballs.

Some **CLOUDS** are more than **10 miles** (16 km) **TALL.**

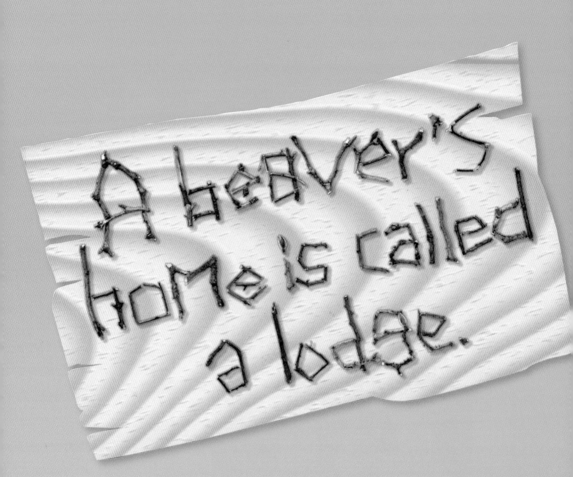

A beaver's home is called a lodge.

94

SATURN HAS MORE THAN 60 MOONS.

It takes **three liters** of freshwater to make **one liter** of bottled water.

COULD YOU SPEAK UP?

A **praying mantis** has only **one ear.**

The north pole of **Uranus** gets no **sunlight** for about **42 years** at a time.

ALL OF THE PEOPLE ON EARTH

COULD CROWD INTO HALF
THE COUNTRY OF BELGIUM.

THE WORLD'S BIGGEST ROCK, **ULURU** IN AUSTRALIA, IS TALLER THAN A 114-STORY BUILDING.

A **geep** is part **goat,** part **sheep.**

There are
more pets in
Japan
than children.

SMELLING GOOD SCENTS, SUCH AS **ROSES,** WHEN YOU SLEEP MAY GIVE YOU **HAPPY DREAMS.**

A goldfish will turn **gray** if kept in the **dark** for a long **time.**

ANCIENT GREEKS USED **hula hoops.**

About 95 percent of the stuff in the universe is invisible.

HORSES CAN TRAVEL UP TO (160 km) 100 MILES IN A DAY.

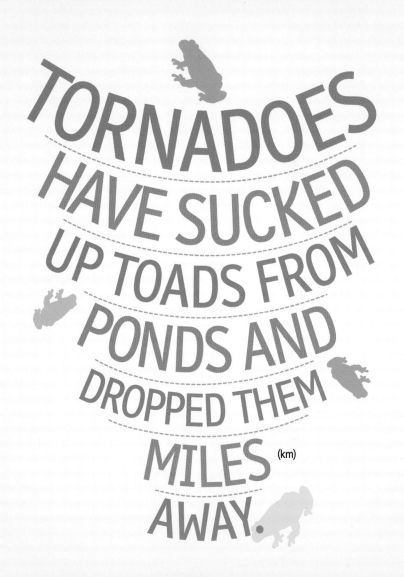

TORNADOES HAVE SUCKED UP TOADS FROM PONDS AND DROPPED THEM MILES (km) AWAY.

A group of jellyfish is called a **smack.**

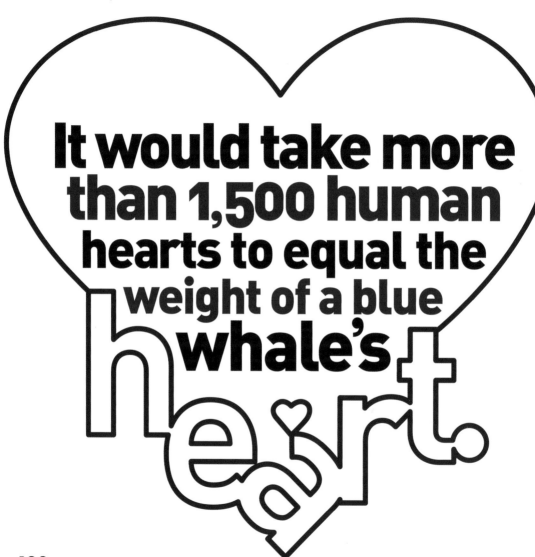

It would take more than 1,500 human hearts to equal the weight of a blue whale's heart.

SOME GEESE CAN SOAR TO 32,000 FEET—
(9,750 m)
HIGH ENOUGH TO SEE A 747 PASSENGER JET FLY BY.

The surface of the moon is smaller than Asia.

OUR UNIVERSE HAS NO CENTER.

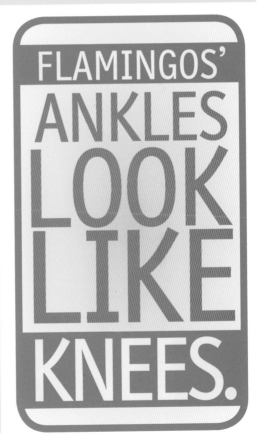

FLAMINGOS' ANKLES LOOK LIKE KNEES.

The oldest **koi fish** lived to be **230** years old.

A **ROCK PYTHON** CAN LIVE FOR A YEAR WITHOUT A MEAL.

THERE ARE VOLCANOES INSIDE SOME GLACIERS.

It's impossible for turtles to stick out their **tongues.**

YOU CAN BUY SOAP THAT SMELLS LIKE BACON FRYING.

A hamster's teeth never stop growing.

THE OLDEST KNOWN **PINE TREE** IS MORE THAN **5,000** YEARS OLD.

▲ **FAN FACT!** SUBMITTED BY ISABEL M., 8

Some of the most expensive **rocks on Earth** come from the **moon.**

A GIRAFFE HAS THE SAME NUMBER OF NECK BONES THAT YOU DO: SEVEN.

Dogs pant up to 300 times a minute.

A group of rhinos is called a crash.

A company in India made a

58-FOOT-WIDE (17.7-m)

pair of underpants—
that's wider than three large SUVs.

Ants have lived on Earth for some 140 million years.

A man in Canada can balance 17 spoons on his face at once.

A rooster is also called a **chanticleer.**

CHEWING GUM WHILE TAKING A TEST **MAY IMPROVE YOUR TEST SCORE,** ACCORDING TO ONE STUDY.

A canary **can sing two different songs** at the same time.

RAW TERMITES TASTE LIKE PINEAPPLE.

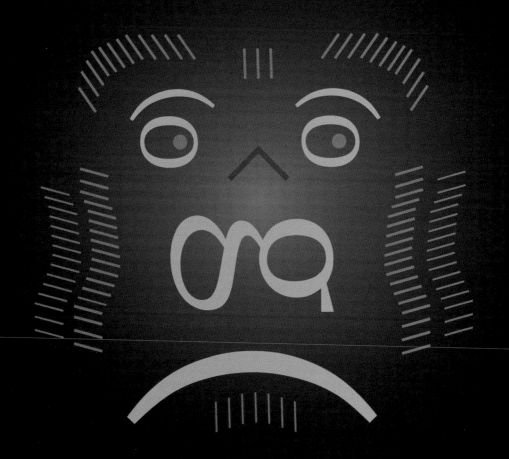

The scientific name for a gorilla is *Gorilla gorilla.*

The
star-nosed
mole
can find
and eat a
snack
in **230**
milliseconds—
faster than
any other animal.

ZUUL CRURIVASTATOR, a newly discovered species of dinosaur, **was named for an evil monster in the** _1984 MOVIE GHOSTBUSTERS._

A TRAIN in Sweden was named **TRAINY McTRAINFACE.**

At Dubai Miracle Garden in the United Arab Emirates, a **full-size model of a jet is covered in** more than 500,000 flowers and living plants.

A FAMILY OF GEESE got a POLICE ESCORT WHILE WADDLING DOWN A HIGHWAY in Colorado, U.S.A.

"SMART BILLBOARDS" IN JAPAN **CAN TARGET ADS AT SPECIFIC DRIVERS.**

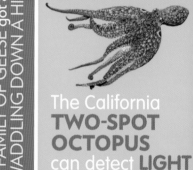

The California **TWO-SPOT OCTOPUS** can detect **LIGHT** with its **SKIN.**

ART STUDENTS IN TAIWAN **MADE POPSICLES FROM POLLUTED WATER** TO RAISE AWARENESS ABOUT POLLUTION.

The MAORI PEOPLE of NEW ZEALAND refer to the WETA INSECT as **"THE GOD OF UGLY THINGS."**

CUCAMELON = a grape-size fruit that looks like a watermelon

THE PEOPLE IN **BRITAIN** DRINK **60 BILLION** CUPS OF TEA EVERY YEAR.

During the 1930s, LIBRARIANS **DELIVERED BOOKS ON HORSEBACK** to people in rural KENTUCKY, U.S.A.

That's Weird!

In the **19th century,** HOCKEY PLAYERS USED **SQUARE PUCKS.**

EATING PUMPKIN SEEDS helps **OSTRICHES** get rid of **PARASITES.**

Some fish eggs hatch in the dad's mouth.

Honeybees have hair on their eyeballs.

YOUR SENSE OF **SMELL** IS WEAKER IN THE MORNING **AND STRONGER IN THE EVENING.**

Sneakers dipped in **18-karat gold** once sold for **$4,053.**

VOLCANIC ERUPTIONS CAN CARRY DIAMONDS TO THE EARTH'S SURFACE.

A man once made

956

pancakes
in one hour.

YOUR
**TONGUE
PRINT**
**IS AS
UNIQUE**
AS YOUR
**FINGER-
PRINTS.**

131

Goats' **eyes** have **rectangular pupils.**

A British **man ate** 36 cockroaches **in 1 minute.**

SOME
SPIDERS
CATCH
AND
EAT
FISH.

One of the world's most expensive coffees comes from animal droppings.

Birds
don't
sweat.

Wombat

waste is cube-shaped.

Paul the octopus correctly predicted that Spain would win the 2010 World Cup.

A SALMON'S SENSE OF SMELL IS THOUSANDS OF TIMES BETTER THAN A DOG'S.

Baby **alligators bark** when they are ready to hatch **out of their eggs.**

A group of **seagulls** is

called a squabble.

Some parrots dance when they hear music.

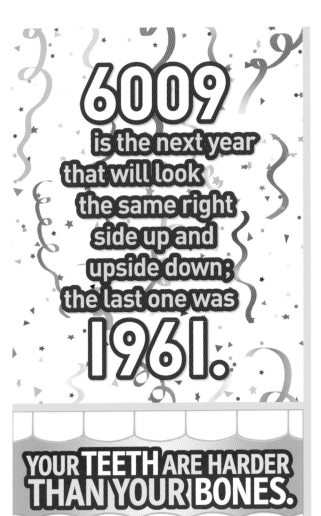

6009 is the next year that will look the same right side up and upside down; the last one was **1961.**

YOUR **TEETH** ARE HARDER THAN YOUR BONES.

An inventor created a cell phone that recharges on Coca-Cola.

A housefly can turn somersaults in the air.

An inventor created **edible** dinner plates.

FAN FACT! SUBMITTED BY JOSHUA A., 11

A tightrope walker is

A restaurant in Taiwan serves **food** in bowls shaped like **toilets.**

A 57-year-old ball of twine weighs **19,000** pounds— (8,618 kg) that's heavier than three hippopotamuses!

called a funambulist.

141

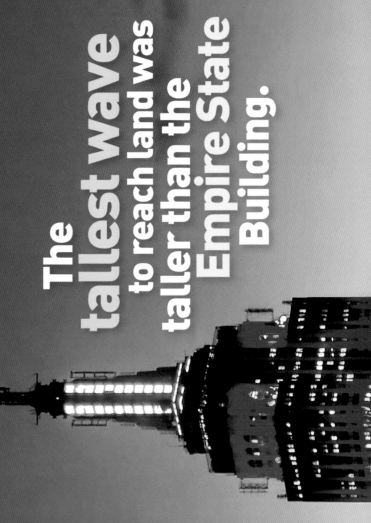

The tallest wave to reach land was taller than the Empire State Building.

142

HERRING COMMUNICATE BY PASSING GAS.

An **ortanique** is a cross between a **tangerine** and an **orange.**

300 MILLION YEARS AGO, SIX-FOOT-LON (1.8-m)

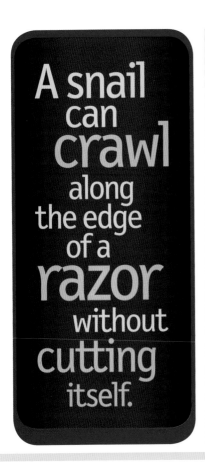

A snail can **crawl** along the edge of a **razor** without **cutting** itself.

MOSQUITOES
PREFER TO BITE PEOPLE WITH
SMELLY FEET.

MILLIPEDES ROAMED THE EARTH.

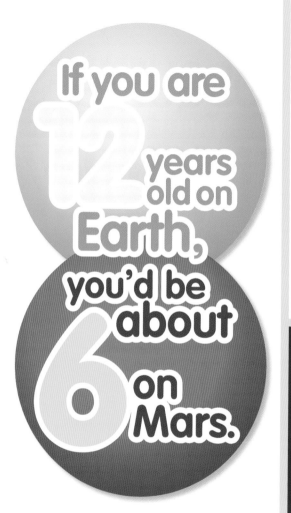

If you are **12** years old on **Earth,** you'd be about **6** on **Mars.**

Some **tree snakes** **glide** up to **78 feet** (24 m) through the air. THAT'S THE LENGTH OF TWO LARGE SCHOOL BUSES.

Mexico City has sunk **26 feet** (8 m) in the last **100 years.**

You can buy an inflatable TV screen.

A VOLCANIC ERUPTION in 1883 made the SUN LOOK GREEN.

The temperature on the moon can be hotter than boiling water.

THE
**DEAD
SEA**
IS SEVEN
TIMES
SALTIER
THAN THE
OCEAN.

Tiny bugs live in your eyebrows.

FAN FACT! SUBMITTED BY MARVIN P., 8

Saturn would float in water.

Some pigs are afraid of mud.

Male seahorses give birth.

APPLES FLOAT BUT PEARS SINK.

More than **70%** of the **Earth's surface** **is water.**

Early golf balls were stuffed with bird feathers.

LARGE FOREST FIRES CAN CREATE TORNADOES MADE OF FLAMES.

▲ FAN FACT! SUBMITTED BY JESSICA M., 9

153

A **fifteen-year-old** cat has probably spent **ten years** of its life **sleeping.**

A giant fungus in Oregon, U.S.A., spreads out over an area the size of 20,000 basketball courts.

Some monkeys in Thailand teach their young to floss.

FAN FACT! SUBMITTED BY EMILY E., 11

MALE PLATYPUSES
CAN STING YOU
WITH THEIR
FEET.

CANADA

99999   99999

FINE GOLD 100 KG OR PUR

THERE ARE SOLID GOLD, **PIZZA-SIZE** CANADIAN COINS WORTH **ONE MILLION** CANADIAN DOLLARS.

LAWS IN ENGLAND

WERE WRITTEN **IN FRENCH** FOR MORE THAN

400 YEARS.

Bat hair HAS BEEN USED AS money.

FAN FACT! SUBMITTED BY TAYMAR W., 14

A Russian man drove a **tractor** more than **13,000 miles** (20,900 km) **in 19 days**—that's longer than the distance from London, England, to Los Angeles, California, U.S.A.

SOME VILLAGES IN POLAND HAVE MORE STORKS THAN PEOPLE.

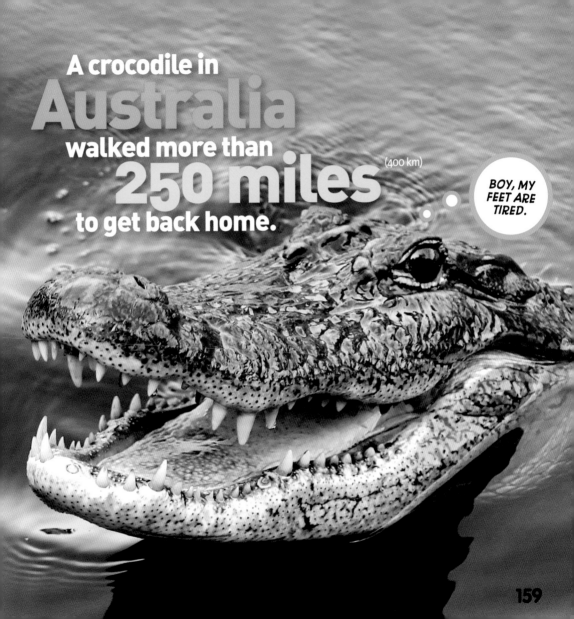

A crocodile in **Australia** walked more than **250 miles** (400 km) to get back home.

BOY, MY FEET ARE TIRED.

ANTARCTICA

IS A DESERT.

A Finnish man wrote a novel

made up of

1,000 text messages.

You can shine your shoes with a banana peel.

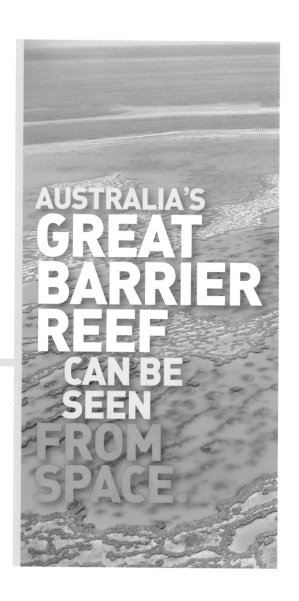

AUSTRALIA'S **GREAT BARRIER REEF** CAN BE SEEN FROM SPACE.

Cold stars are red.

Hot stars are blue.

Some lizards can **walk on water.**

An artist in New York City opened a **CONVENIENCE STORE** made entirely of **HANDMADE FELT PRODUCTS.**

For **$1,400** you can buy an **18-karat-gold** bracelet shaped like the **LEAFY VEGETABLE KALE.**

The **BRIDE** of a **WORLD WAR II SOLDIER** had her **WEDDING DRESS** made from a **PARACHUTE** that **SAVED HER HUSBAND'S LIFE.**

A group of **STINGRAYS** is called a **FEVER.**

THE SUN LOSES 4.6 MILLION TONS (4.2 million t) **OF ITS MASS EVERY SECOND.**

When they're feeding, **SEAHORSES** make the **SOUND OF LIPS SMACKING.**

OTTAWA, CANADA, hosts winter **DRAGON BOAT RACES** on the ice.

An OFFICIAL U.S. POSTAGE STAMP features a **TOTAL SOLAR ECLIPSE** that **CHANGES TO A MOON** when you put your finger on it.

Your **SHOELACE KNOTS WITHSTAND MORE FORCE WHEN YOU RUN** than your body does when you're **RIDING A ROLLER COASTER!**

SCIENTISTS DESIGNED A ROBOT that **EXTRACTS VENOM from SCORPIONS.**

The **MOROCCAN FLIC-FLAC SPIDER** travels by doing **CARTWHEELS.**

That's Weird!

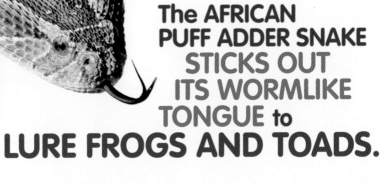

The **AFRICAN PUFF ADDER SNAKE STICKS OUT ITS WORMLIKE TONGUE** to **LURE FROGS AND TOADS.**

You can buy
bat droppings
for about
$10
a pound.

Chewing gum while peeling onions may keep you from crying.

The **tallest** known living **man** is **8 feet,** (246 cm) **1 inch tall—**

a foot and a half (45.7 cm) **taller** than an average pro **basketball player.**

IT TAKES 8 MINUTES AND 19 SECONDS FOR LIGHT TO TRAVEL FROM THE SUN TO EARTH.

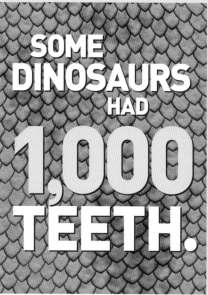

SOME DINOSAURS HAD 1,000 TEETH.

ADULTS HAVE AS MANY AS 1,500 DREAMS A YEAR.

Bees can be green, blue, or red.

A farmer in **Lebanon** grew a **25-pound potato.** (11-kg) That's the weight of two bowling balls!

FAN FACT!
SUBMITTED BY CARLY L., 11

171

The world's largest **swimming pool,** in Chile, **stretches for half a mile.**

(0.8 km)

A **flamingo** can eat only when its head **is upside down.**

A HOUND DOG NAMED TIGGER HAD EARS THAT WERE EACH

14 INCHES LONG—

(35.6 cm)

THAT'S LONGER THAN TWO OF THESE BOOKS SIDE BY SIDE.

Almonds belong to the rose family.

FAN FACT! SUBMITTED BY MCKENZIE B., 12

FAN FACT! SUBMITTED BY HAILEY H., 11

A company once sold insurance that covered people in case of injury from a falling coconut.

SOME MAKEUP HAS FISH SCALES IN IT.

BABIES' CRIES CAN SOUND DIFFERENT IN DIFFERENT LANGUAGES.

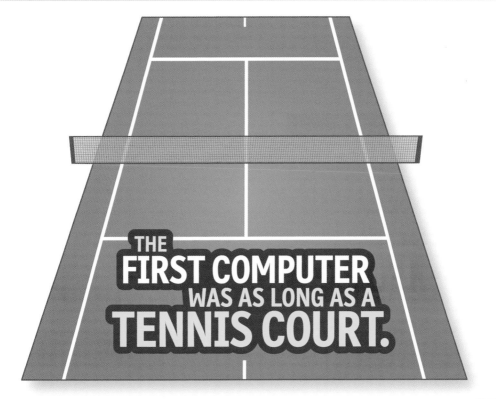

THE FIRST COMPUTER WAS AS LONG AS A TENNIS COURT.

The sound of waves crashing comes mostly from air bubbles.

A Scottish dish called haggis is cooked inside a sheep's stomach.

Rainbow-colored grasshoppers live in the rain forests of Peru.

A TRAFFIC JAM IN CHINA LASTED

You can buy **worms** from a vending machine in Japan.

FOR MORE THAN A WEEK.

Ferrets have been used to carry **television cables** through pipes in Europe.

THE SHORTEST PROFESSIONAL **BASEBALL PLAYER** WAS **3** FEET, **7** INCHES (109 cm) **TALL,** THE HEIGHT OF AN **AVERAGE 5-YEAR-OLD.**

If you never **cut your hair,** it would likely stop growing at about **two feet long.** (61 cm)

SOME **BIRDS** CAN USE THEIR **BILLS** TO MEASURE THE TEMPERATURE OF THEIR **NESTS.**

A **MAN** DRESSED AS **SANTA CLAUS** WENT **SKYDIVING** OVER THE **NORTH** POLE.

Half the world's oxygen is made in the ocean.

YOU ARE MORE LIKELY TO BE IN A BAD MOOD ON THURSDAYS, ACCORDING TO ONE STUDY.

Brain cells live longer than all of the other cells in your body.

A FIVE-SEAT BICYCLE IS CALLED A **QUINDEM.**

THERE ARE MORE SPECIES OF BEETLES ON EARTH THAN OF ANY OTHER CREATURE.

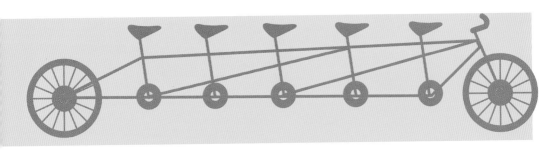

A BUILDING IN POLAND LOOKS LIKE IT'S MELTING.

AN EARTHQUAKE **IN CHILE** SHORTENED THE LENGTH OF AN EARTH **DAY** BY 1.26 MICROSECONDS.

THE LENGTH of YOUR FOOT is about EQUAL to

the DISTANCE FROM your ELBOW to YOUR wrist.

There is no time at the center of a black hole.

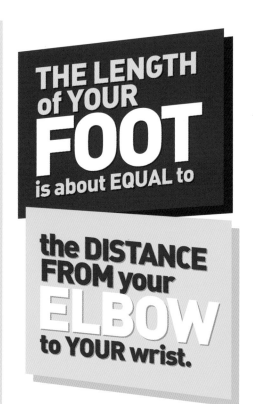

FAN FACT! SUBMITTED BY MILES J., 10

L A C H A N O P H O B I A

is the fear of vegetables.

YOU CAN COMPETE IN AN underwater mountain bike race

IN WALES, UNITED KINGDOM.

A sailfish can leap through the air at 68 miles an hour— (109 km/h) **that's about the speed a car drives on the highway.**

THERE ARE ABOUT

70

LAKES

HIDDEN UNDER THE ANTARCTIC

ICE.

Leeches can live in your nose.

Some baby birds use claws on their wings to climb trees.

There are
mushrooms
that glow
in the
dark.

PUG + BEAGLE

PUGGLE

Rotten
eggs
float in
water.

BARBIE'S PETS

HAVE INCLUDED A
LION, PARROT, AND GIRAFFE.

FAN FACT! SUBMITTED BY AUDREY LU M., 14

You can write about 45,000 words with an average pencil.

Penguins swim up to **3,100 miles** in a year. (5,000 km)

THE INFORMATION STORED ON AN **iPOD NANO** WOULD FILL UP **EIGHT PICKUP TRUCKLOADS** OF PAPER.

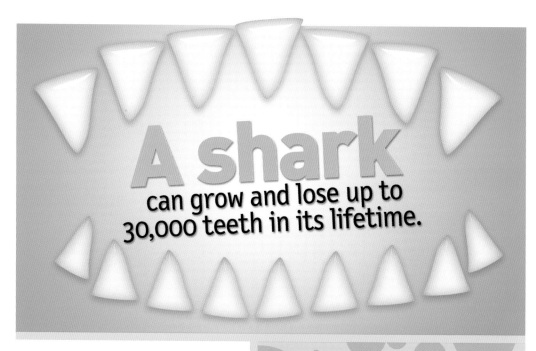

A shark can grow and lose up to 30,000 teeth in its lifetime.

HARMLESS MICROSCOPIC SHRIMP MAY LIVE IN YOUR DRINKING WATER.

Some artists use chewing gum to make paintings.

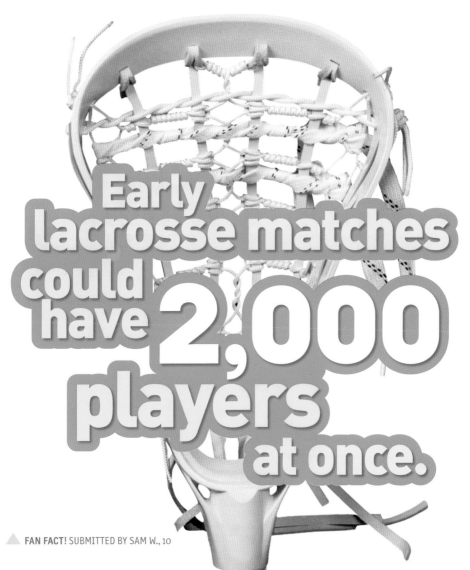

Early lacrosse matches could have **2,000** players at once.

A British
candy company created
a giant box of
chocolates filled with
220

052

individual candies.

There is a
museum devoted to
ramen noodles
in Japan.

FAN FACT! SUBMITTED BY AIDAN C., 9

SOME TURTLES BREATHE THROUGH THEIR REAR ENDS.

FAN FACT!
SUBMITTED BY
ANNA M., 8

Woodpeckers once pecked holes in the space shuttle.

BALD EAGLES CAN SWIM.

Some dinosaur eggs weighed more than 10 pounds.

(4.5 kg)

A BIRD CALLED THE ARCTIC TERN FLIES MORE THAN A MILLION MILES (1.6 million km) **IN ITS LIFETIME—**

THAT'S THE SAME DISTANCE AS MAKING THREE ROUND-TRIP FLIGHTS TO THE MOON.

FAN FACT! SUBMITTED BY ZAID A., 11

Circus workers call the toilet a doniker.

It takes **713 GALLONS OF WATER** (2,700 L) to make one cotton T-shirt.

ZOOKEEPERS
ARE BITTEN

MORE OFTEN BY ZEBRAS THAN BY TIGERS.

▲ **FAN FACT!** SUBMITTED BY RORY AND KIERNAN F., 10

A Chinese man can **blow up balloons** using his **ears.**

It's not possible to TICKLE yourself.

207

GUESS WHAT?

A house flew two miles into the air! **HOW?**

Crocodiles eat rocks! **WHY?**

Pluto Platter is the original name of this popular, well-known toy! **WHAT?**

WANNA FIND OUT?

The FUN doesn't have to end here! Find these far-out facts and more in *Weird But True! 4.*

NATIONAL GEOGRAPHIC KiDS

AVAILABLE WHEREVER BOOKS ARE SOLD
Get a fun freebie at natgeokids.com/fun-pack

FACTFINDER

Boldface indicates illustrations.

A

Aboriginals 80
African cicadas 42
African puff adders 165, **165**
Air bubbles 178
Airplanes 13, **13,** 83, **83,** 124, **124**
Alaska, U.S.A.
 ice outhouse 44
 sand dunes 25, **25**
Alligators 135
Almonds 176, **176**
Antarctica 90, 160–161,
 160–161, 190
Ants 63, 118, **118**
Apples 152, **152**
Arctic terns 203
Asparagus 45, **45**
Astronauts 16, 44, 56, 59, 81
Aztec 12

B

Babies: cries 177
Bacon 113, **113**
Bacteria 51
Bald eagles 201
Balloons 206, **206**
Bamboo sharks 44, **44**
Banana peels 162, **162**
Barbie (doll) 194

Baseball 18, **18,** 182
Basketball players 169, **169**
Bats 158, 166, **166**
Batteries 84
Beagles **192**
Beavers 94
Bees 25, 127, **127,** 171, **171**
Beetles 60, **61,** 185
Belgium 97, **97**
Bicycles 31, 184, **185,** 189
Birds 133, 182, 190
Black holes 188, **188**
Black lights 25
Black mambas 42
Blinking 64
Blondes 58
Blue (color) 71, **71,** 163
Blue whales 47, 108
Bombardier beetles 60, **61**
Bones 36, 70, 115, 139
Books 84, 125
Bowls, toilet-shaped 141
Brains 31, **31,** 36, 184
Bread 85
Breathing 69, 200
Bridges 84, **84**
Britain: tea drinking 125
Brunettes 58
Bugs: in eyebrows 150
Burping 83
Butterflies 51, **51**

C

Cables, television 180
California two-spot octopuses
 124, **124**
Camels 47, 70
Canada
 gold coins 157, **157**
 red river 66, **66–67**
Canaries 120
Catnip tea 56, **56**
Cats 32, 44, 154, **154–155**
Cell phones 84, 139
Cells, brain 184
Cheetahs 38
Chewing gum 120, **120,** 167, 196
Chile
 earthquake 188
 world's largest pool 172, **172**
Chimpanzees 51, 86–87, **87**
Chocolate 12, 71, 198–199, **198–199**
Chromophobia 89
Circus workers 203
Clouds **10–11,** 18, **18,** 45,
 92–93, 93
Coca-Cola 139, **139**
Cockroaches 132
Coconut crabs 84, **84**
Coconuts 176
Coffee 132, **132**
Coffee-pot-shaped tower 84, **84**
Color vision 62, 79
Colors, fear of 89

209

Computer, first 177
Corpse flowers 40, **40–41**
Crabs 84, **84**
Cranberries 42
Creativity 71
Crocodiles 65, **65**, 159, **159**
Crying 167
Crystals 43, 45, 52, **52**
Cucamelons 125, **125**
Cupcake-shaped handbag 43

D

Dead Sea **148–149**, 149
Diamonds 14, **14**, 76, **76**, 128
Dinner plates 140, **140**
Dinosaurs 53, **53**, 58–59, 124, **124**, 170, 202
Dogs
    breeds 192–193, **192–193**
    long ears 174, 175
    panting 115
    sizes 15
    space travel 56
Dolphins 48, **48–49**, **86**, 86–87
Doughnuts 20, **20**
Dragon boats 164, **164**
Dreams 102, 170
Dresses 84, 164, **164**
Droppings, animal 14, 132, 134, 166
Dubai Miracle Garden, United Arab Emirates 124, **124**

E

Eagles 52, 201
Ears 32, **174**, 175, 206
Earth
    atmosphere 11
    core 22
    length of day 24, 188
    light from sun 170
    spinning speed 9
    surface 152
    temperature 50
    weight 12
Earthquakes 69, 188
Eclipses 165, **165**
Eggs
    alligators 135
    bees 25
    dinosaurs 202
    fish 126
    rotten 194, **194**
Egypt, ancient 47
Electricity 14
Elephant seals 85, **85**
Elephants 12, 14, 33
Elevators 45
England
    laws 157
    swans 91
Everest, Mount, China-Nepal 50, **50**
Extinct species 54–55

Eyebrows 64, 150, **150**
Eyelashes 64
Eyelids 47
Eyes
    blinking 64
    camels 47
    goats 132
    hearing them move 91
    honeybees 127, **127**
    spiders 90

F

Fabric 44, **44**
Facial expressions 37, **37**
Feathers 152
Feet 18, **18**, 82, 145, 157, 188
Ferrets 180, **180–181**
Fingerprints 131, 138
Fish 102, **110–111**, 111, 132, 189, **189**
Fish eggs 126
Fish scales 176
Flamingos 109, 173, **173**
Flossing 157
Flowers 40, **40–41**, 59, **59**, 124, **124**
Forest fires 153
French (language) 157
Friday the 13th 83
Frogs 12, 26, 36, 165
Funambulists 140–141
Fungus, giant 156

G

Garbage 7
Garlic 56, **56**
Gas, passing 144
Geeps 100
Geese 109, 124
Giraffes **10**, 115, 194
Glaciers 112, **112**
Glow-in-the-dark mushrooms 191, **191**
Goats 100, 132
Gold
    amount of mined gold 19
    Canadian coins 157, **157**
    gold-plated bicycle 31
    kale-shaped bracelet 164
    600-pound nugget 88, **88**
    sneakers dipped in 127, **127**
Goldfish 102
Golf balls 152, **152**
Gorillas 121
Grand Canyon, Arizona, U.S.A. 37
Grasshoppers 178, **178**
Great Barrier Reef, Australia 162, **162**
Greeks, ancient 102
Guinea pigs 52, **52**
Gum 120, **120**, 167, 196

H

Haggis 178
Hailstones 91
Hair
    bats 158
    honeybees 127, **127**
    humans 12, 58, 64, 82, 182
Hamburgers 90, **90**
Hamsters 114, **114**
Hawaiian alphabet 64
Hearts 5, 14, 25, 108
Herring 144
Hippopotamuses 65, **65**
Hockey pucks 125
Honeybees 127, **127**
Horses 104, **104–105**, 125
Hot chocolate 12
Hotels 7
Houseflies 139
Hula hoops 102
Humpback whales 77

I

Ice
    lakes under 190
    lollipop-shaped crystals 45
    outhouse made of 44
    in Saturn's rings 31
Ice cream 56
Icebergs 74, **74**
Inflatable TV screens 147

Insect species: rain forests 46
Insurance 176
International Space Station 59
iPod Nano 195

J

Japan
    noodle museum 200
    pets 101
    "smart billboards" 124
    strawberries 45, **45**
    vending machines 179
Jell-O 16
Jellyfish 107, **107**
Jupiter (planet) 21, **21**

K

Kale-shaped bracelet 164
Kangaroos 6, **6**
Koi **110–111**, 111

L

Lachanophobia 188
Lacrosse 197, **197**
Laika (dog) 56
Lakes 75, 190
Languages 68, 177
Latte art 44, 85, **85**
Laws 157

FACTFINDER

Leeches 190, **190**
Lemons 8, **8**
Lenticular clouds 18, **18**
Librarians 125
Light, speed of 170–171
Lightning 57, **57**
Lions 194
Lizards 28, **28–29,** 163

M

Mailboxes 81, **81**
Makeup 176
Mantis shrimp **78–79,** 79
Marble runs 85
Mars (planet) 146
Menorahs 69, **69**
Metal detectors 88
Meteorites 81
Mexico City, Mexico 146
Milk 77, **77**
Millipedes 144–145
Mir (space station) 16, **17**
Moctezuma (Aztec ruler) 12
Money 76, 157, **157,** 158
Monkeys 157
Moods 184
Moon 50, 109, **109,** 115, 147,
   165
Moroccan flic-flac spiders
   165
Mosquitoes 145

Moths 33
Mountain bike race, underwater
   189
Mucus 52
Mud 150
Mummies 47, **47**
Muscles: cats' ears 32
Museums 44, 200
Mushrooms 191, **191**

N

Neck bones 115
Nests 52, 182, **182**
Niagara Falls, Canada-U.S.A.
   34–35, 35
North Pole 56, 183
Novels 162

O

Ocean 149, 183
Octopuses **4–5,** 5, 124, **124,**
   135, **135**
Olive oil 56
Onions 167, **167**
Ortaniques 144, **144**
Ostriches 125, **125**
Outhouses 44
Oxygen 183

P

Paddleboarding 44, **44**
Pancakes 129, **129**
Parachutes 164
Parasites 125
Parrots 82, **82,** 138, **138,** 194
Parthenon replica: Germany 84
Pears 152, **152**
Pencils 194, **194**
Penguins 195, **195**
Pet spas 56
Pets 44, 45, 101, 194
Pigs 150
Pine tree, oldest known 114,
   114
Pineapples 120, **120**
Pizza 30, **30**
Platypuses 157
Poland
   "melting" building **186–187,**
      187
   storks 158
Pollution 124
Popcorn 27, **27**
Popsicles 124, **124**
Postage stamps 165, **165**
Potatoes 171, **171**
Praying mantises **44,** 95, **95**
Puggles **193**
Pugs **192**
Pumpkin seeds 125

Q

Queen bees 25
Queen of England 91
Quindems 184, **185**

R

Rain forests 46, 178
Rainbow-colored grasshoppers
178, **178**
Rainbows 26, **26**
Ramen noodles 200, **200**
Rats 45, **45**, 83, **83**
Red (color)
diamonds 76, **76**
and heart rate 14
river 66, **66–67**
stars 163
teams wearing 7
Restaurants 90, 141
Rhinoceroses 116, **116–117**
Rivers, red 66, **66–67**
Robots 165
Rock pythons 112
Rocks 31, 37, **98–99**, 99, 115
Rome (place name) 47
Rome, Italy: hotel 7
Roosters 119, **119**
Roses, scent of 102
Running 12, 165

S

Sahara, Africa 75, **75**
Sailfish 189, **189**
Salmon 135
Salt 76
Sand dunes 25, **25**
Santa Claus 183
Saturn (planet) 31, **31**, 95, 150
Scorpions 25, 165
Sea stars 63, **63**
Seagulls 136–137, **136–137**
Seahorses 84, **84**, 151, **151**,
164, **164**
Seaweed 84, **84**
Selfies 44
Sharks 33, **33**, 44, **44**, 71
Sheep 100, 178
Shipwrecks 84
Shoelace knots 165
Shoes 127, **127**, 162, **165**
Shrimp **78–79**, 79, 196
Skin 51, 58, 124
Skunks 58, **58**
Skydiving 183
Sleep 48, 102, 154
Smell, sense of 29, 127, 135
Smells 40, 102, 113
Snails 145
Snakes 42, 112, 146, 165, **165**
Sneakers, gold-dipped 127, **127**
Snow 37

Soap, bacon-scented 113
Solar eclipses 165, **165**
Space shuttles 83, **83**, 201, **201**
Space stations 16, **17**, 59
Space travel 56, 59
Sperm whales 31
Spiders 90, 132, 165
Spit 56
Spoons 119, **119**
Star-nosed moles 122, **122–123**
Stars 163
Stingrays 164, **164**
Stomachs 52, 178
Storks 158
Strawberries 8, 45, **45**
Sugar 8
Sun 76, 96, 147, 164, 165,
165, 170
"Sun" (word) 44
Swans 91
Sweating 18, 133
Swimming
bald eagles 201
penguins 195, **195**
Swimming pools 85, 172, **172**

T

T-shirts 203
Taiwan 69, 124, 141
Tallest man 168, **168**
Tea 56, **56**, 125, **125**

213

FACTFINDER

Teeth 114, 139, 170, 196, **196**
Termites 120
Test scores 120
Text messages 162
Tickling 207
Tigers 204–205, **205**
Tigger (dog) **174,** 175
Tightrope walkers 140–141
Time 188
Toads 106, **106,** 165
Toilets 141, 203
Tongue prints 131
Tongues
    lizards 28, **29**
    puff adders 165, **165**
    turtles 113, **113**
Tornadoes 106, 153
Tractors 158
Traffic jams 178–179
Trains 124
Tree snakes 146
Turtles 113, **113,** 200
Twine 141, **141**

U

Uluru Rock, Australia **98–99,** 99
Underpants 118, **118**
United States
    first airplane journey across 13
    postage stamp 165, **165**
Universe 6, 103, 109

Uranus (planet) 96, **96**
Urine, recycled 81

V

Vegetables, fear of 188
Vending machines 30, **30,** 179
Venom 165
Vesuvius, Mount, Italy 85
Volcanoes 112, 128, 147

W

Wales: underwater bike race 189
Wars, shortest 7
Warthogs 76
Water
    bottled 95, **95**
    Earth's surface 152
    in human brain 36
    microscopic shrimp 196
    polluted 124
    from recycled urine 81
Water towers 84, **84**
Water use 95, 203
Waterfalls **34–35,** 35
Waves 142, 178
Wedding dresses 164, **164**
Whales 31, 47, 77, 108
Winter 26, 164
Wombats 134, **134**
Woodchucks 70

Woodpeckers 201
World Cup (2010) 135
World population 73, 97
World War II 164
Worms 179

Y

Yawning 51
Years: the same right side
    up and upside down 139

Z

Zebras 39, **204,** 204–205
Zookeepers 204–205
Zuul crurivastator 124, **124**

PHOTO**CREDITS**

Cover (giraffe), prapass/Shutterstock; spine (giraffe), jaroslava V/Shutterstock; 2, prapass/Shutterstock; 4-5 (RT CTR), Vittorio Bruno/Shutterstock; 6 (RT), Dave Long/iStockphoto.com; 7 (UP LE), Shutterstock; 7 (LO CTR), iStockphoto.com; 9 (CTR), Shutterstock; 9 (CTR), Jonathan Halling; 10-11, Andrejs Zemdega/iStockphoto.com; 14 (LO CTR LE), badahos/Shutterstock; 17 (CTR), NASA; 18 (LO RT), NASA; 19, Frank and Helena Herholdt/cultura/Getty Images; 20 (LE), Michael Flippo/iStockphoto.com; 21 (CTR), NASA; 22-23, kavram/Shutterstock; 25, Nick Jans/Alaskastock.com; 27 (CTR), Jonathan Halling; 28-29, Stephen Shaw/iStockphoto.com; 34-35, Nikola Bilic/Shutterstock; 40-41, Andrew Ward/Life File/Photodisc/Getty Images; 43, Ruth Black/Shutterstock; 44 (UP LE), Peter Unger/Getty Images; 44 (CTR LE), Brian Overfelt; 44 (LO LE), Sana Studio/Shutterstock; 44 (UP RT), NASA; 44 (LO RT), Doug Perrine/NPL/Minden Pictures; 45 (UP LE), Hong Vo/Shutterstock; 45 (UP RT), Kyodo/Newscom; 45 (LO), Sonsedska Yuliia/Shutterstock; 48-49 (RT), Debra McGuire/iStockphoto.com; 52 (UP LE), Igor Dutina/iStockphoto.com; 53 (CTR), Franco Tempesta; 56 (UP RT), Andrey Stenkin/iStockphoto.com; 57 (CTR), Glenn Kasner/National Geographic My Shot; 59 (LO LE), Kesu/Shutterstock; 60-61 (RT CTR), Satoshi Kuribayashi/Nature Production/Minden Pictures; 63 (UP RT), David Pruter/iStockphoto.com; 64 (LO CTR), Rob Friedman/iStockphoto.com; 65 (CTR), Vaclav Silha/Barcroft USA Ltd; 66-67, Solent News/Rex/Rex USA; 70 (LO RT), Shutterstock; 72-73, dbimages/Alamy; 74, Rob Broek/iStockphoto.com; 75, Giorgio Fochesato/iStockphoto.com; 76 (UP LE), J. Helgason/Shutterstock; 78-79, Image Focus/Shutterstock; 80, pamspix/iStockphoto.com; 82 (UP RT), Rogerio Mathias/National Geographic My Shot; 84 (UP LE), divedog/Shutterstock; 84 (UP RT), GOLFX/Shutterstock; 84 (LO LE), Janos Rautonen/Shutterstock; 84 (LO CTR), Michele and Tom Grimm/Alamy Stock Photo; 84 (LO RT), Barisev Roman/Shutterstock; 85 (UP), AFP/Getty Images; 85 (LO), David Osborn/Shutterstock; 86 (UP LE), Winston Link/Shutterstock; 86, Ramunas Bruzas/Shutterstock; 87 (UP RT), iStockphoto.com; 87, Igor Karon/Shutterstock; 88 (CTR), Matthew Benoit/Shutterstock; 90 (LO CTR LE), nycshooter/iStockphoto.com; 92-93, Robert Ranson/Shutterstock; 95 (LO LE), thumb/iStockphoto.com; 96, David Aguilar; 98-99, Art Wolfe; 104-105, Revonda Gentry/National Geographic My Shot; 109 (UP LE), Brad Thompson/Shutterstock; 110-111, Torsten Wittmann/iStockphoto.com; 113 (UP CTR), Melissa Brandes/Shutterstock; 114 (LO LE), Eric Isselée/Shutterstock; 114 (LO RT), Mike Norton/iStockphoto.com; 116-117, Karel Gallas/Shutterstock; 118 (LO CTR), Mark Moffett/Minden Pictures; 119 (LE), Nick Schlax/iStockphoto.com; 119 (RT), Aksenova Natalya/Shutterstock; 120 (UP RT), YinYang/iStockphoto.com; 122-123, Kenneth C. Catania; 123, Robert Dant/iStockphoto.com; 124 (LO LE), 100%純污水製冰所 (Pure Sewage Water Ice Making); 124 (LO RT), Tobias Bernhard/Getty Images; 124 (CTR LE), Francesco Bonino/Shutterstock; 124 (UP RT), Norbert Wu/Minden Pictures; 125 (UP RT), Alison Thompson/Alamy Stock Photo; 125 (UP LE), M. Unal Ozmen/Shutterstock; 125 (LO), Anan Kaewkhammul/Shutterstock; 127 (UP CTR), Manfred Kage/Peter Arnold Images/Photolibrary; 127 (LO RT), Koji Yano/courtesy www.justanotherrichkid.com; 130-125, Neustockimages/iStockphoto.com; 130-131, Kateryna Moskalenko/Shutterstock; 134, Keiichi Hiki/iStockphoto.com; 136-137 (LO RT), ALEAIMAGE/iStockphoto.com; 139 (LO RT), Karin Lau/iStockphoto.com; 141 (LO CTR RT), Jonathan Halling; 142-143, gary718/Shutterstock; 144 (UP CTR), HelleM/iStockphoto.com; 144 (RT CTR), University of California Riverside; 147 (RT), sandsun/iStockphoto.com; 148-149, AlexGul/Shutterstock; 151, Rudie Kuiter/oceanwideimages.com; 152 (LO RT), Dan Thornberg/iStockphoto.com; 154-155, Kati Molin/Shutterstock; 157, Tom Hanson, CP/Associated Press; 159, iStockphoto.com; 160-161, Gordon Wiltsie/NationalGeographicStock.com; 160, Andrew Winning/Reuters//Corbis; 162 (RT), KJA/iStockphoto.com; 164 (UP LE), Lucy Sparrow; 164 (LO RT), Rich Carey/Shutterstock; 164 (CTR), National Museum of American History & Smithsonian Institution Archives; 164 (LO LE), Bert Hoferichter/Alamy Stock Photo; 164 (UP RT), © 2008 Samantha T. Photography/Getty Images; 165 (LO), iStock photo/Getty Images; 165 (UP LE), Courtesy the United States Postal Service; 165 (UP CTR LE), Courtesy the United States Postal Service; 165 (UP RT), Trong Nguyen/Shutterstock; 166, Barry Mansell/naturepl.com; 166, Marek Mnich/iStockphoto.com; 168, Andrew Winning/Reuters; 169, Noah Graham/Getty Images; 171 (RT), spxChrome/iStockphoto.com; 172, Reuters/Crystal Lagoons/San Alfonso del Mar; 173, David Hsu/Shutterstock; 174, Karine Aigner/NGS Staff; 176 (UP LE), iStockphoto.com; 176 (UP RT), Vibrant Image Studio/Shutterstock; 178, angelo gilardelli/iStockphoto.com; 180-181, Dmitry Grivenko/Shutterstock; 183 (RT CTR), idreamphoto/Shutterstock; 186-187, PhotoBliss/Alamy; 189 (LO CTR), Darren Pearson/iStockphoto.com; 190 (LO RT), Michael Gray/iStockphoto.com; 191, Takeshi Mizukoshi/Pacific Press/Photo Researchers, Inc.; 192 (LE CTR), Andrew Johnson/iStockphoto.com; 192 (RT CTR), Eric Isselée/iStockphoto.com; 192 (CTR), Bonnie Schupp/iStockphoto.com; 194 (LO RT), Uyen Le/iStockphoto.com; 194, Franco Tempesta; 195 (UP CTR), Corbis Super RF/Alamy; 197, Brian Palmer/iStockphoto.com; 198-199, imagedepotpro/iStockphoto.com; 201 (LE), NASA; 204, Ivan Liakhovenko/Shutterstock; 205, Don Bayley/iStockphoto.com

215

Since 1888, the National Geographic Society has
funded more than 12,000 research, exploration,
and preservation projects around the world.
The Society receives funds from National
Geographic Partners, LLC, funded in part by
your purchase. A portion of the proceeds from
this book supports this vital work. To learn
more, visit natgeo.com/info.

For more information, visit
nationalgeographic.com, call 1-877-873-6846,
or write to the following address:

National Geographic Partners
1145 17th Street N.W.
Washington, D.C. 20036-4688 U.S.A.

Visit us online at nationalgeographic.com/books

For librarians and teachers:
ngchildrensbooks.org

More for kids from National Geographic:
natgeokids.com

For rights or permissions inquiries, please
contact National Geographic Books Subsidiary
Rights: bookrights@natgeo.com

Designed by Rachael Hamm Plett, Moduza Design

First edition published 2011
Reissued and updated 2018

Trade paperback ISBN: 978-1-4263-3108-4
Reinforced library binding ISBN:
978-1-4263-3109-1

The publisher would like to thank Jen Agresta,
project manager; Robin Terry, project manager;
Julie Beer, researcher; Michelle Harris,
researcher; Paige Towler, project editor; Eva
Absher-Schantz, art director; Julide Dengel,
art director; Kathryn Robbins, art director;
Ruthie Thompson, designer; Lori Epstein,
photo director; Hillary Leo, photo editor;
Anne LeongSon and Gus Tello, production
assistants.

Printed in Hong Kong
23/PPHK/3